C0-ATH-191

Learning to Foxtrot

Learning to Foxtrot

Barbara Unger

The Bellevue Press

PS
3571
.N44
L4
1989

The author wishes to thank the following publications in which these poems first appeared: *The Albany Review* for "Learning to Foxtrot" and "Silverware," *Buckle* for "Housewife," *Carolina Quarterly* for "Sonya," *Contact II* for "A Female Aesthetic" and "Another Poetry Handbook," *Footwork* (Passaic County Community College) for "Wreckage," *Frontiers: A Journal of Women Studies* (U. Colorado: Boulder) for "Near Kent Falls," *The Greenfield Review* for "New Year's Eve," *Inprint* (North Shore Community College) for "At the Single's Social" and "On the High Wire," *Invisible City* for "She-Child I," *Laurel Review* for "The Double," *The Massachusetts Review* for "The Snakeskin," *Minnesota Review* for "Woman Professor," *The Nation* for "Geological Faults," *Off Our Backs* for "Cold Wash," *Oxalis* for "The Crone Poem," *The Pale Fire Review* for "Ruth" and "After Hawthorne's 'Rappaccini's Daughter'," *Poet & Critic* for "Corn Maiden," *Poetry Now* for "The Abortion," *Quixote* for "She-Child II," *Southern Humanities Review* for "Penelope," *Sparrow* for "Requiem for a Lady," *The Spirit That Moves Us* for "Riding The Penn Central into New York City," *St. Andrews Review* for "The Dream Thief," "Scheherazade, the Wife," and "Sharing a Lover," *Stone Country* for "Cassandra on Eighth Avenue," *Twigs* for "New Milford Waterhole," *Wind* for "To my Father," and *Wisconsin Review* for "Breasts."

The following poems appeared in anthologies: "Mother and Daughter" and "Sister Catherine" in *I Name Myself Daughter and it is Good* (Sophia Books: Columbus, Ohio, 1981) ; "Exposure" in *National Poetry Foundation Winners, 1982* (Chester Jones National Poetry Foundation, 1982) ; "Breasts" was reprinted from *Wisconsin Review* in *Disenchantments: An Anthology of Modern Fairy Tale Poetry* (University Press of New England: Hanover and London, 1986) ; "Riding The Penn Central into New York City" was reprinted from *The Spirit That Moves Us* in *The Spirit That Moves Us Seventh Anniversary Issue* (Iowa City, Ia., 1979) ; "Geological Faults" was reprinted from *The Nation* in *American Yearbook of Magazine Verse 1981-82* (Monitor Books: Beverly Hills, Calif., 1982) and "Silverware" will be reprinted from *The Albany Review* in *American Yearbook of Magazine Verse 1989-90* (Monitor Books: Beverly Hills, Calif., 1989).

Some of these poems were included in a manuscript that won a Goodman Award from The Thorntree Press in 1989.

Copyright © 1989 by Barbara Unger

ISBN 0-933466-06-4

21134248

This book is for my husband, Ted Sakano.

The author wishes to thank the University Awards
Program of The State University of New York,
The Ragdale Foundation, New York State Council
on the Arts, and The Rockland Center for the
Arts for grants which enabled her
to complete this book.

Contents

Late Knocking

Netting the Flesh

Learning to Foxtrot

We are all virgins again
spell *God* without an *O*
graceful in our bodies
never growing old.

In the slam book they call me
prettiest, you most popular.
You blonde your hair,
I stuff my bra,

Sing bawdy sailor songs
sotto voce in Wednesday assembly
while the boys fly
the wild blue yonder.

We crouch under desks
safe from bombs,
belly-crawl beneath
the beach obstacle course.

Hand around your waist,
starched middies crush
familiar breasts,

We two-step backwards,
quarrel over who leads,
take turns being the girl.

Mother says *don't frown.*
Smile and God will notice.
Your face is your fortune.

Learning to Foxtrot

The real war is in the mirror
until a distant Asian city
melted, shook flesh from bone,
dwarfing our razed retreats
as whole cities went under in hell.

Near Kent Falls

Matched in the crawl,
both loving
Ingrid Bergman,

Our page boys flat
in pincurls
under rubber caps

Our linked hands
above water,

We counted off
to the lifeguard's whistle
in summer camp.

Muscles tread
bicycle curves
kicking up sunnies
in our slipstream
off the slippery bottom.

The year everyone married
we threw showers,
compared china patterns
and towels.

We had no time.
Each of us had a father
waiting to give us away.

At my reception,
sore feet flung from pumps,

Near Kent Falls

We clung,
counting off numbers,
holding each other up safely
for the last time
before we went under.

Requiem for a Lady

There's a big five-and-ten
in your eyes, girl,
and with your waddle,
you're the Empress of All China.
Besides, all the soup's
inside you, though gladiolas
bloom between your irises.

I didn't think
you married
the way
the nun
in you
came from Darien,
wouldn't cry.

I say
black litanies
for you
in the Aquarium.

Among school children,
plaid scarves mingling,
Brighteyes,
I think I see you,
bemused, sitting
atop the stone lions
outside the Library.

She-Child I

daughter
dwelled in mud
wavy as a himalaya,
your unstable movement
knobby-kneed on swings
is not

child of culotte,
iron teapot, swing,

Klee-wild
doodling-up
the golden sun
crushing the weight
of my smile
with the blue
winding-spool
of what will be

your dissident
clam-clay mould
revolutionary of the IS
in all the star-filled
prayer books

when I
bellyful of hippopotamus
bore you river-wild
down the white Euphrates
and met the nightblue
tides of the Tigris.

She-Child II

... and bore you? What
woman on an elephant,
British-type, sun helmet,
white ducks and all,
was I?

Order of successive montage
you come, a unit of stars
and impose no savage tropic
on all the dawn world
of cookbook and clock.

Woman's fiction be you not.
livid as lobster
you were
the antelope and tiger
that graze.

The Crone Poem

In bed I wear
black lace
to hide her
from you,

The woman who wrings
gizzards and necks
into her heaped apron

Tangerine beaks
dangle from her
carmine hands,

The fishwife who squats,
baiting her hook.

Look, soon we will be ruddy
as their glistening bellies.

Turn away from her.

If you saw her
you would know
your oldest enemy.

No woman
will be safe
in your arms.

Cold Wash

Grinning navels
contorted in a sexual fury
of mated color and foam.

Rainbow blur thrashes
past the black window.

Like a sated belly dancer
the turbine grinds
to a chromatic stop.

Gradually colors formulate,
relax into separate identities,
printed shirts, patched jeans,
stained jockey shorts,
Disney pajamas
bodies tranquil
in vicarious orgasm.

From the black womb
contents pour out,
placenta-like
into the plastic bag.

Compulsively I mate socks.
Backbreaker! Lawsamercy!
Women's work is never done.
My life is defined
by the computerized shriek
of the Stop cycle.

The mesh basket,
like the Mafia,
collects its daily payoff.

New Milford Waterhole

Songs of glistening bees,
murmurings of restless lovers
rise and fall in the drone
of untutored harmonicas and guitars
in the loamy dust of a campus summer.

Elongated shadows of tanned lovers
flicker in firelit haunts,
exchanging shimmers of oiled flanks,

White-breasted girls of August
shake out their drying locks
while on the factory side
in sullen shadows from scaffolding
stemming the muddy tide
grey-faced mothers dangle
swollen feet, dogs dive,
yelping as they enter the river.

Old men of some dustbowl color nod,
heads down, hands the color of clay,
watch an alluvial sun
beat down into the bronze of hay
the glistening hair of the girls
of this last campus summer,
their wounded backs turned,

Girls of this goodbye summer
turned like strangers
fleeing a conquered city.

Housewife

She waits
at the edge of her body
where the boundaries never change.

Outside fat bustling houses
with lit windows,
tidy or untidy inside.

These are the bones
that net the flesh.

Mountains jump out,
rude clowns,

Lawns mock her,
yards of turf
outlaw her nightly,
exhaling taffeta sighs,

While she bangs kettles
on electric coils,
a nightmare man creeps
like a slug
through the trees.

She sees him pass
her child's window
wearing her shimmering
old boots,

Dim in the moonlight,
a trampling Cossack
smashing her vines.

The Double

Scheherazade, the Wife

Once my nights were spent
beneath billowing tents of illusion,
postponing denouements,
outwitting executions.

But now, more wife than entertainer,
I'm the good one who listens.

Waterbearer emptying the cup
as the bells of the sun jangle,
it crawls on its belly,
thirsty camel, bent spoon
always some new twist,

Melodrama exchanged
for mysteries of the nuptial bed.

Only this plot without interruption,
the languor of constant surprise.

Still Scheherazade is the Sultan's favorite,
clever at never repeating herself.

Come, I whisper,
lie between my legs.
Tell me my future.

Sister Catherine at Big Sur

On the other side of the glass,
a nun imagines herself
naked on a bicycle
with only one wheel.

The sky collects snow,
grey miser,
won't open its palm.

She pedals
her defective machine
and won't let go,

For the flesh
is made of air
and spins
on invisible spokes.

She struggles
through white drifts
as she rides
God's body
like a bronze Godiva,

Then falls.

Everything that sinks
must rise.

I shake
the paperweight.

Snow everywhere.

Cassandra on Eighth Avenue

She walks
the streets
licks and bites
lifts her skirts
plays dunces
dances on luck
dropped out of the sky,

Demands your watches
and gold chains
coaches Maria
who paints her nails
before the suicide
tells you Heaven's
the place you can buy
Jack Daniels cheap,
nothing can be that bad
when they build
cities on the stars.

Her monster
never sleeps.

Its bed will
always be ready.

Some things never change.

Woman Professor

My English teacher
writes me letters
in pink Flair
lengthier
than my essay.

Meanwhile
I am quietly inciting
a revolution of words
a seduction machine
subtler than Mao or Marx.
I am captivating
a woman accustomed
to Lawrence and Keats.
What an opportunity
for the Snake!

She summons it up
against the menopause
ticking like a clock
in the arena of the page.

Meanwhile
like an unwritten poem
she cuddles me
against her breast
though my words expire
shoved away in a drawer
only *Fair,* a *C*+
in the marking book
of her heart.

I am resurrected much later
in her new course,
Social Change and Literature.

Exposure

His second wife
feeds the guppies
that bob around the mothers
in the green aeration
of his desk aquarium,

Separates the predators,
watchful for brownouts
and power failures
to a fragile ecosystem.

I want to instruct her
on phone numbers, dentists,
watchmakers, caterers,

Itemize his faults
to the last detail.

She may learn to endure
one or two
spectacular devourings

While she dusts the photo
of three children
faces still tender
as he prefers,
forever pubescent
and out of danger.

How cleverly she angles it
to evade the dazzling sun
distanced from the tank's
glassy artifice.

Exposure

I am in the picture too,
a woman wearing a lacquered beehive.

Sun splits our faces.

Corn Maiden

What is the Corn Maiden
doing in my closet?
A tassel of gold
like a watchfob
on her nose,
pollen on her cheek,
among the linens
counting the pillow cases?

Why is the Creation Miracle
changing the birth order
of the universe
hanging towels
over the bars,
decorating soap?

Watch, Coyote,
your plan is disrupted.
Rain falls in the shower.
The dog barks.
You mourn
in the tub,
saving face.

Ruth

Naomi leads and I follow.
We can't talk — women
who sew up our hearts
in prickly places.

Orpah was smart,
strapped her rucksack on,
hitched back
to her home town.

Bad luck to those
who left us.
Sore feet, no harvest.

But here the land lies low and level,
just right for the thirsty willow.
These hands are strong.
I'm not afraid to darken them
threshing wheat.

Beneath the moon's bitten core
Naomi's voice taunts me:
*In your land
you had nothing.*

Here one needs
cherish soup,
survival bones.

So when her kinsman Boaz pinions me
with his eyes, I slip my shawl
to the earthen floor,
coil my hips and smile.

The Double

There were good times
in spite of the double
I traced for a disaster.

The double is paper-thin,
nothing does her in.

A stitched bald head
rests on her shoulders.
Even Christ cannot resist
her pure ashen flame
stealing oxygen.

Discovering the taste of Braille,
the invention of blood,
an obvious leaning
on the other,

I wear her under my coat
smooth as the belljar
on a Japanese terrarium.

Only a gun moll
or a foreign spy
can detect the outline.

An easy fit,
she can be worn
to an auto da fé
or a public execution

Perfect doubles,
we'll never split.

Her wild eye
courts you
like a woman in love.

To my Father

I stole your armor
your iron suit, lance,
face guards, epaulettes,
and put them in the museum
under the Tower
where I secretly practiced
wearing them,

Even perfected
your signature
on my death warrant.

Then I saw you in the glass Tower
wondering if you could see me
without my iron vest
or red wig, imagined
letting your severed head
bleed over my velvet robe.

After Hawthorne's "Rappaccini's Daughter"

A conundrum,
this deadly thumb
that snaps off
doomed heroes.

Oh that it had
turned black
before my body's
curious burning . . .

Common scolds safekeep
lovers in their beds
while I husband only
these gem-like pods.

Even pot herbs wilt
in their stuffy kitchens,
domestic rot.

Town girls, their beds
on borrowed time, kneel
to bless themselves

When they spy
my brown figure
trowelling the rows.

Poisonous flowers
thrill to my freak touch.
Crippled, they need
no camouflage.

In the green glut
of this dread arcana
my gift spares nothing.

Penelope

In this house
even common objects
can be made to sing
in perfect pitch.

He has returned the lost spoon
from the wedding silver.
Everything shines in its own hunger,
even the flayed skins of the suitors
iridescent on my silent looms,

Those he slew for me.
There were many, even babies
whose voices grew to be human.

It was good for a time
to be rid of the skeleton of habit.
Now we make love warily,
listen to the domestic drip,
the refrigerator hum. To him
I am still the homecoming queen
awash in grandstand noise —

He, the clever imposter
who lifts my hips to join him.
It's a kind of home,
not quite what he dreamed of.

Husband, we have not been far
from here. Now we are home.

Snakeskin

The Dream Thief

Your double
the sad priest
who averts his eyes
won't shake my hand
is never pleased.

You cannot love
a broken oracle
the unwired colossus
you climb
to scrape out lies.

Even your melancholy choirs
cannot pull him through.

Red scarf over her brow,
my double
trudges through sugar fields
doing battle with cane,
slashing stalks
below the root
where belief
is sub-tropical.

Her machete swings
in the dangerous dance
to which she is wedded.

The sadness these doubles feel
is an empty field in autumn
where apples cluster.

I let you feast on them
fathering the fall.
I let her whirl,
paper target
on a bed of straw.

Their appetites are vast,
their hands huge,
capable of anything.

New Year's Eve

Wrong exit on the Thruway
and the AM dial brings
only traffic fatalities.
Only place still open,
BeverageMart on Route 9.

The announcer talks of Lennon.
No assassinations this year.

Snow seeps inside my skull,
a white cranial cavity.

No signs I hoped to find.
Silence flows like milk
into cold metal cans.

Do I exist? Are you the mountain?
Am I climbing you? If I fall
will they find me here
frozen into radioactive crystals?

I snap off the radio dial
and dig myself into a silence
deep as a snow bank,

Mine the only car
on this road tonight
as it escapes into the Catskills,
fringe of violet trees
blurs to inky ribbon.

I should be invisible,
sipping cocktails
at a smart city pub

Instead of studying
how the absence of light
bruises the gothic phantasm
of rural America,

Somewhere between
Red Hook and Elizaville.

At the Single's Social

A man wants to leave his wife,
hires a hall, a band of musicians,
spares no expense.

Under electric stars
he describes
the cameo perfection
of a woman he once loved.

I slide into the arc
of his outstretched arm—
he shuffles me,
a cut deck.

Moisture crescents my silk
as he thrusts
a polyester leg
between mine,
masterful
tango turns.

That's when I notice a wall
of discarded women
no longer young.
One bares her teeth,
her cat eyes follow
my snakey foxtrot.

At the coatroom
I watch her:
yesterday's tiger bloom,
tonight's wilted streamer.

In this hall of strangers,
touch is everything.

Riding The Penn Central Railroad into New York City

West on the Hudson's
nuclear radiance
pleasure craft dot the river.

The Palisades
enclose the Western shore.

White wake of a motor boat
reminds her of the picnics
of last summer.
She can still taste
the salt spray
on her lips.

Now she rides alone
to the broken city.
Bankrupt train creeps
along the water's edge
into the slums of The Bronx.

Last week kid terrorists shot
the man in the first car.
Today they only hurl bottles,
shattering a window or two.
There is talk of bullet-proof glass.

Forward is freedom
through the dark tunnel.
What can you sacrifice,
woman,
freedom
rider?

Wreckage

Lovers
who fear
closeness

We skim
depths
romp
like playful sharks
always
near the surface

Until U-boats
from old newsreels
torpedo in
riddling
our divers' suits
with holes.

We hang on
to the detritus
of our lives

While our history
floats
recklessly by
like the dead
for whom nothing matters.

Sharing a Lover

I slice you thin
make do with shavings
of ice or skin,

Play at winter love,
razors
singing in my head.

Frugal as a wolf
I'm an unwilling convert
who huddles with squatters
on a cold chapel floor,

My ration of mystery
warm with communal taste.

An Eskimo squaw
I set out on the sled
dragging you behind,
then hatchet the line
to leave you
on the ice floe

Adrift,
in the frozen boat
of your name.

The Snakeskin

You saved the snakeskin
in a bag of alfalfa sprouts.

Diamond sheath
in brown-grey,
it seemed sheer
as the stocking

Of a woman,
the kind
known best
in the dark.

No country girl, I
don't come from a town
where women offer their silence
to a spoon or plate.

Stroke me
as you would
silk.

This is the mystery of blood,
the splitting open of birth,

The magical skull
that reproduces from its own seed,
dreaming itself petals,
stamens, pistils.

In its envelope
the skin of the snake
shivers in anticipation,
waiting for night to fall.

Lost in Elizaville

Ahead a clothesline of Yule lights
festoons a farmhouse, crippled pickup
in the driveway. Electricity from uranium
flows into Christmas bulbs.
I knock, asking directions.

Embarrassed, the man explains
my botched turn, lets me use the phone.

A woman with dancer's legs cries
into the sink above music of The Sixties
blaring from the stereo,

Her freckled arm flung
against the light
that hurts her eyes.

The man revs up the truck
and waves. I get into my old car
as if I'm the one afflicted,

Shiver to hear ice let go,
a dream of bushels
here smashed
just outside
the city's sprawl,

The homely sounds
of Peter, Paul and Mary

... whatever it is
they sing about
behind me.

Lights flicker on and off
all over the Hudson Valley.

Late Knocking

Breasts

Sisters
Snow White and Rose Red
you are the two
sides of the coin
Mother tossed up
for luck
landing heads first.

Held up
between the fingers
you are
erect flesh to contend,
two soldiers
in mini-skirts

Or for
ladypoets to stuff
soggy tissues
between, tear-stained.

Pillows to stroke,
dugs to be sucked,
jellyfish to spawn,

Tugging us back
again and again
into our own mothers,
beginning, drying, dying.

Mouths that clutch arms
and some primal Mother
that encircles us all
like a tree that fissures
out of the center of all things.

Sonya

Steam in the samovar.
Father returns from Paris
with talk of revolution.
men laughing
their heads off
starched cousins
from the Caucasus.

But the escape artist
is Momma writing letters.
For a time the family
must stay behind.

Sonya hides
under thick woolen petticoats
of her Nanya, threatens
not to cross an ocean alone.

                    *

Lurch of the ship
influenza floating
above steel basins,
a grey vapor.

What fault
has brought her here
to this? Without
Nanya's damp earth smell,
Momma's silks and hand-sewn borders
stuffed with patchouli?

                    *

At Castle Gardens,
Port of New York,
children without parents
form a charity line.

The American lady
gives out free handkerchiefs,
red, white and blue
like flags with machine-made hems
and itchy stars.

Sonya pans the pavement
with gunmetal eyes.
You are a crooked needle, Sonya,
sew straight.

No gold in the streets,
nothing free
in America.

Mother and Daughter

We rise in the dark   meet in the kitchen
two women in bathrobes   sharing dreams

All night I am making the beds
on my knees   tucking in sheets   folding
hospital corners   oblivious   to your

Upturned wrists   two bleeding ribbons
Can one survive? *Never mind*   I say
an ordinary affair   *such wounds are minor*
and I return to plumping pillows

Watching the traveling star   as dawn streaks
through the straw blinds   coffee steams

On the yellow stove   in this messy kitchen
we laugh   two women in dirty bathrobes

Sharing dreams   one day   we will fold
into each other's scars   opening each

Like a petal   as you sleep   in your lover's arms
in other cities   dreams no one dare disturb.

The Abortion

At seventeen she wants
only what's supportable
in the body's business,

Who believed her monthly blood
a reliable oasis.

It was no worse,
she swears, than slicing onions
or the dentist's drill,

But her eyes are flecked
with tiny black scars
and shiver like eggs
in porcelain cups.

I mourn her lost baby teeth,
her thirsty sprouting.

This summer at camp
she cares for six-year-olds,
carries them piggy-back
up Girl's Hill,

Snuggles them in her bedroll
after light's out,

Cradles them against
her flannel hip
when they cry out
Mother
in their sleep.

A Female Aestheic

symbols
anthropology
fairy tales
the old matriarchy

the Bly prediction
of the return of the
four-pronged Mother,
the good of it.

no surprises.

American Indian Lit. Renaissance.
a symbolic return
to the Great Mother.
ecology.
defense of earth.

see Sexton's *Transformations*
as such an effort
to re-tell the literature
of the Great Mother.

Kali/Mary/
Eve/Grendel/

forgotten energies.

If a woman understands a poem
　　it itches under her fingernails.

If a woman lives with a poem
　　it roots in her dresser.

If a woman lives with two poems
　　one of them misunderstands her.

If a woman gets angry at a poem
　　she waters a plant shoot.

If a woman publicly denounces poetry
　　the food on her table will spoil.

If a woman gives up poetry for power
　　she shall have lots of power.

If a woman brags about her poems
　　she shall sleep on a circus ground
　　in an empty bathtub.

If a woman denies her poems pleasure
　　she shall beat her child.

If a woman praises the poem of a sister
　　her kitchen streams with sunlight.

If a woman overly praises the poem of a sister
　　they will quarrel in cold weather.

If a woman claims the poem of another
　　her larder will be bare.

If a woman's poems go naked
　　she will bury a lover.

Geological Faults

Geological faults
and other wonders
invade my fossil dreams.
He and I stand
on the Columbia Ice Cap
Canadian tourist trap
testing the queer blue ice
the kind they say runs deep
miles and miles.

Solid it held us up
above the hot dog concession
and tramway, supporting
hundreds of visitors daily
and Sonja Henie
for years.

Nobody could guess
the adjoining crevasses would swallow
the whole trading post.
The children and I
wear Saskatchewan mittens,
hold palms up bravely
as we slip through
caverns of ice
our costume skirts
tilted upward
like broken umbrellas.

Now on the sunless side of the canyon
I fly alone on my home-made mechanism,
a downy giant bat
frightening lizards
who scuttle under cold rock
afraid of the woman
who fell from the sky.

I soar, dive, touch bottom
then rise again into cobalt blue.
Around my webbed wings
whirls a lasso of buzzards,
moving soundlessly,
waiting for
the thawed wax
the faulty bolt
the broken wing.

On the High Wire

My daughter is gone
in her place a gypsy
who reads Tarot,

An angel on 24-hour duty.

No death, only change
No fate, only play.

The cards are a circus net
in case I crash through,
suspended fifty feet in the air

a blue-spangled figure
teetering on the edge
of my long life-line.

The cards don't lie.

Only come down,
Mother, she says, *come down*
safely. And I do.

Silverware

One devours, one is eaten,
as they say. Don't worry.
I'm neither. I've turned out okay.

It's hard once somebody gets lost
and found again. You've grown accustomed
to a new mother each time,

A kitelady
manipulating the wind
juggler of lives
holding what floats in air
by the finest of blood cords.

Whetstone and blade,
glissando, you see me
through a scrimmage
of lost latchkeys,
blunted affections.

Yet the silverware's safe
in my hands.

At the table we order sparingly,
toast ourselves anew:

The same mother
the same daughter

Alphabet

They're burning down the nursery.
China dolls, wooden blocks,
hold-to-the-light jungles.

Behind the lines in a hut
an old grandmother reads
big letters from a cloth book.

She is teaching me my name.

Daughter,
those wolf teeth
I see in your eyes
are like tentfires
in an alien camp,

This climate we still inhabit—
scorched grassfield
after battle.

Severing the Cord

From California you report in
three thousand miles away,
on this strange malady.

By night you clench to a fetal pose,
wake with muscles strained
as nightmares of domestic wars
march across the combat zone.
I, the family doctor,
expected to heal all hurts,
hysterical as symptoms multiply.

Your bones chafe, muscles groan,
the mirror confirms. This time
no last-minute rescue.

No waiting to outgrow,
for the next stage arriving
in town just in the nick of time
like the cavalry in the old Westerns.

Now it's for good. Everything counts.
This is what I try to tell you,
daughter, and then the cure —

Unclench, relax, stretch
like a young mare embracing the dawn.
Thread yourself into it.
Lock into its turbulence.
Become that woman your bones ache for.
I give you permission.

Tomorrow you'll wake poised for voyage
as I stand on the shore.
That's what mothers are for. I'll say goodbye.
Darling, make the most of it.

Note on the Author

Barbara Unger's poems have appeared in many magazines and anthologies including *The Nation, The Beloit Poetry Journal, Southern Humanities Review, The Massachusetts Review, Carolina Quarterly, Southern Poetry Review, Kansas Quarterly, The Wisconsin Review, Minnesota Review* and anthologies from The University Press of New England and Monitor Books. Three books have appeared: *Inside The Wind* (Linwood Publishers: Stone Mountain, Ga., 1986); *The Man Who Burned Money* (The Bellevue Press: Binghamton, N.Y., 1980) and *Basement Poems 1959-63* (Isthmus Press: San Francisco, Calif., 1975). She is the recipient of grants from The New York State Council on the Arts, The State University of New York, The Squaw Valley Community of Writers, Edna St. Vincent Millay Colony for the Arts, Inc., Ragdale Foundation, and Hambidge Center for the Creative Arts and Sciences. The National Endowment for the Arts helped fund her first book of poetry. A Breadloaf Scholar, Barbara Unger has been nominated for the Pushcart Prize and was a winner in the Chester Jones National Poetry Awards and the West Virginia Poetry Contest. She is a Professor of English at Rockland Community College of The State University of New York. In 1986 she was Writer-in-Residence at Rockland Center for the Arts. She also publishes criticism and fiction. A collection of short fiction is expected in 1990.

Note on the Book

This book is set in Baskerville, a typeface designed by John Baskerville in 1757. 500 copies were printed letterpress by Stuart McCarty at The Geryon Press, Limited, in Tunnel, New York, for The Bellevue Press.

PS 3571 .N44 .L4 1989

Unger, Barbara 1932–

Learning to foxtrot

NOV 9 1990

DEMCO